D0477546

9112000183986

A Child's History of Britain

# Life in Tudor Britain

Anita Ganeri

Text © Capstone Global Library Limited 2014
First published in hardback in 2014
The moral rights of the proprietor have been asserted.

Edited by Nick Hunter and Penny West
Designed by Joanna Malivoire
Original illustration © Capstone Global Library Ltd 2014
Illustrated by: Laszlo Veres (pp.26-7), Beehive Illustration
Picture research by Mica Brancic
Originated by Capstone Global Library Ltd
Production by Helen McCreath
Printed and bound in China

ISBN 978 1 406 27051 8
18 17 16 15 14
10 9 8 7 6 5 4 3 2 1

**British Library Cataloguing in Publication Data**
A full catalogue record for this book is available from the British Library.

**Acknowledgements**
We would like to thank the following for permission to reproduce photographs: © Mary Rose Trust p. 26 bottom; Alamy pp. 8 (© eye35.pix), 9 (© Greg Balfour Evans), 15 top (© Mike Booth), 20 (© Gavin Haskell), 22 (© Image Asset Management Ltd./World History Archive), 23 (Travelshots.com/© Peter Phipp); Corbis pp. 6 (© Corbis), 13 (© The Gallery Collection), 24 (© Lebrecht/Lebrecht Music & Arts), 25 (© Gianni Dagli Orti); Getty Images pp. 5 (The Bridgeman Art Library/English School), 7 (De Agostini Picture Library/G. Dagli Orti), 18 (Hulton Archive), 21 (Hulton Fine Art Collection/British Library/Robana), 26 top (Hulton Archive/Epics); Mary Evans Picture Library pp. 16 (© Mary Evans Picture Library 2010), 17 (© Mary Evans Picture Library 2011), 19 (© Mary Evans Picture Library 2010); Shutterstock p. 15 bottom (© Crepesoles); Superstock p. 11 (Superstock); The Picturedesk pp. 10 (The Art Archive/Marquess of Bath/Eileen Tweedy), 14 (The Art Archive/John Meek); Topham Picturepoint/TopFoto p. 12 (The Granger Collection).
Cover photograph of three Tudor children reproduced with permission of The Bridgeman Art Library (Rafael Valls Gallery, London, UK).

We would like to thank Heather Montgomery for her invaluable help in the preparation of this book.

Every effort has been made to contact copyright holders of material reproduced in this book. Any omissions will be rectified in subsequent printings if notice is given to the publishers.

# Contents

Some words are shown in bold, **like this**. You can find out what they mean by looking in the glossary.

# Tudor Britain

Tudor kings and queens ruled England from 1485 to 1603. At that time, Scotland was a separate, independent country, with its own kings and queens. Edward I, the English king, had conquered part of Wales in 1282. By 1536, the whole of Wales was under English rule.

During the Wars of the Roses, two branches of the same family fought for the English throne. Henry Tudor was from the House of Lancaster. Their **emblem** was a red rose. His rival, King Richard III, came from the House of York, which had a white rose.

In 1485, Henry defeated Richard III at the Battle of Bosworth, and was crowned king. He married Elizabeth of York, uniting the houses of Lancaster and York. A red and white rose became the Tudor emblem, to show that the struggle between the two houses was over.

## TUDOR TIMELINE

| | |
|---|---|
| 1455–1485 | Wars of the Roses |
| 1485–1509 | **Reign** of Henry VII |
| 1509–1547 | Reign of Henry VIII |
| 1547–1553 | Reign of Edward VI |
| 1553–1558 | Reign of Mary I |
| 1558–1603 | Reign of Elizabeth I |

This is a portrait of Henry Tudor, who became King Henry VII.

# Who were the Tudors?

The king or queen was at the head of Tudor society. Below were the nobles and **gentry**. They owned large amounts of land, which made them very rich. Many nobles had country estates, but spent most of their time at the royal **court**. Nobles and gentry had to send soldiers for the **monarch**'s army if there was a war. The Church was also very rich and powerful when Henry VII came to the throne.

The middle level of society included merchants, craftsmen, and successful farmers, called yeomen. There were also educated people, such as doctors and lawyers. They were reasonably well off but most were not rich.

Queen Elizabeth I was the daughter of King Henry VIII.

# A hard life

For most ordinary people in Tudor times, life was hard. Farm workers and servants worked long hours for very little pay. Many people could not find jobs. There were many **vagrants** and beggars, travelling around looking for work.

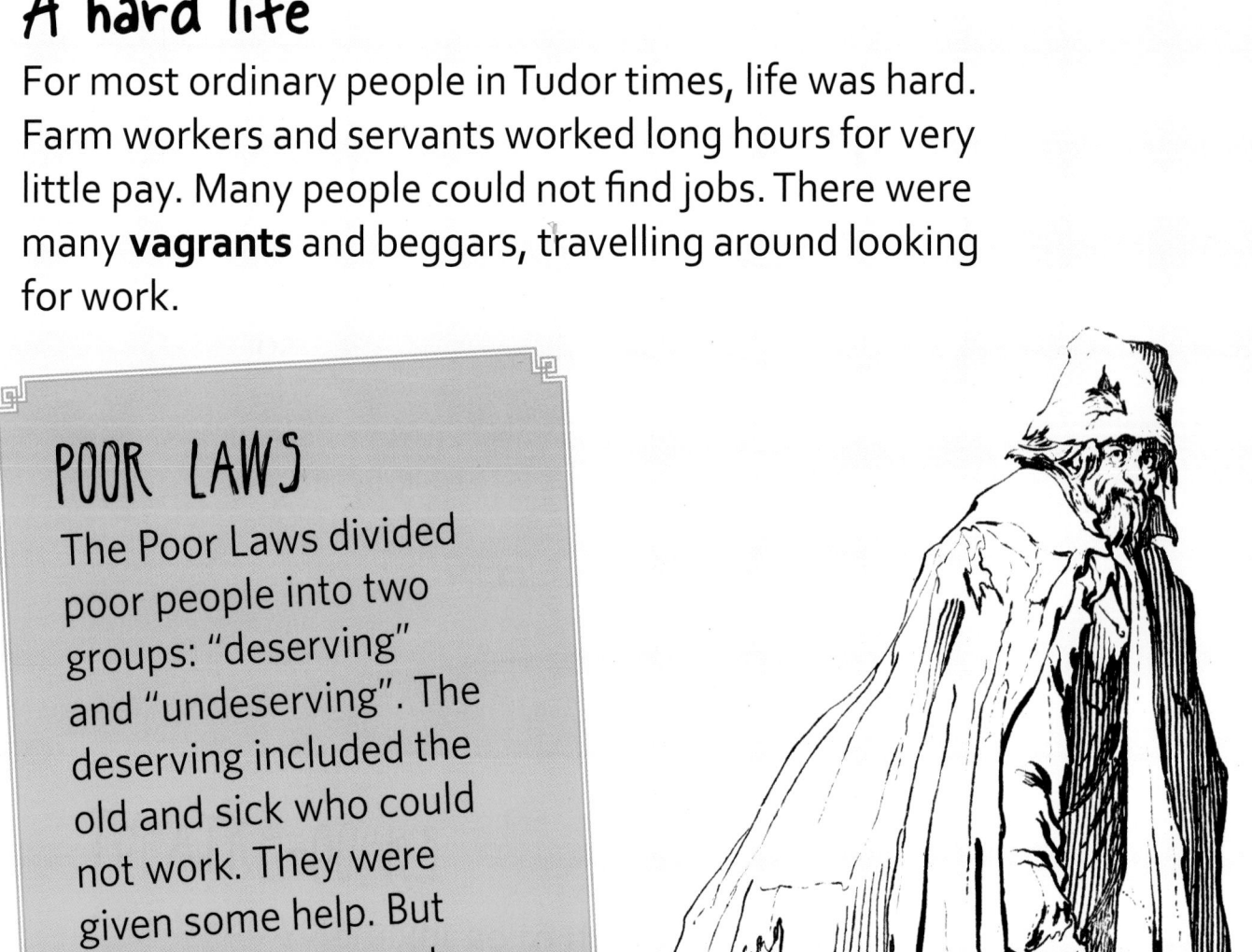

## POOR LAWS

The Poor Laws divided poor people into two groups: "deserving" and "undeserving". The deserving included the old and sick who could not work. They were given some help. But undeserving vagrants and beggars were often punished, and sometimes even executed, if they broke the law.

Beggars were a common sight in Tudor times.

# Where would I live?

If you were a child in Tudor times and your parents were very wealthy, you might live in a grand house. Your house probably had glass in the windows, and large chimneys on its roof. Inside, the rooms often had rich, wooden **panelling** to keep out the draughts.

Hardwick Hall, near Chesterfield in Derbyshire, took seven years to build in the 1590s.

## TUDOR LONDON

In 1500, there were around 50,000 people living in London. By 1600, this number had grown to 200,000. The city was very overcrowded. Compared to London today, it was tiny – you could walk from the middle of the city to the countryside in 20 minutes!

Thatched, half-timbered cottages can still be seen in England.

Many merchant families lived in "half-timbered" houses. A half-timbered house got its name from its wooden (timber) frame. The spaces between the frames were filled in with bricks or with wattle and daub – woven twigs covered with plaster to make a smooth wall.

For children from poorer families, home was often a small house with just one or two rooms. You had very little furniture, perhaps a few wooden benches, stools, and tables. Richer people could afford better furniture, often made out of oak. Furniture, such as beds or chests, was handed down from one generation of a family to another.

# What would my family be like?

This is a painting of a wealthy Tudor family, with their many children.

In Tudor times, your family was very important, whether you were rich or poor. People often had more children than they do today. They needed children to look after them in their old age and to carry on the family name. Sadly, many children died at a young age because the Tudors knew little about how to prevent and cure diseases.

# A full house

Your household probably included your parents, your grandparents, aunts, uncles, and cousins. Wealthy families also had plenty of servants to look after them. Tudor parents were very strict. You were expected to obey your parents and might be beaten if you did something wrong.

Up to the age of seven, most children were looked after by their mothers or older brothers and sisters. After this, if you came from a poor family, you had to start work. In wealthy families, some boys went to school. Girls were expected to learn the skills they needed to run a home.

## MARRIAGE

In Tudor times, children could get married when they were as young as 12, though most people married in their twenties. All Tudor couples got married in church.

This painting shows the celebration meal after a Tudor wedding.

# What clothes would I wear?

If you were poor, you wore hard-wearing clothes made from rough wool cloth. Boys wore **breeches** tucked into woollen leggings, with a wool or linen shirt. Girls wore a fitted top and long skirt over linen petticoats. Both girls and boys covered their heads when they went out. Girls tucked a linen cap over their hair. Boys had woollen caps.

These peasants need hard-wearing clothes to plough the field.

# High fashion

In rich families, people could afford clothes made from fine woollen cloth, cotton, or silk. At **court**, nobles wore the latest and most expensive fashions. Men wore tight-fitting breeches, called hose, with silk shirts and doublets (jackets). Women wore full skirts over frames made of whalebone or wood. Both men and women wore frilly linen collars, called ruffs, around their necks.

There were strict laws in Tudor times about what people could wear. For example, only the **gentry** or nobles were allowed to wear velvet or silk.

## JEWELS AND DECORATIONS

Wealthy Tudors wore clothes decorated with jewels, and **embroidered** with gold and silver. These fabulous outfits were a way of showing off how rich and important they were. We know a lot about these clothes from paintings of the time.

This is the famous explorer Sir Walter Raleigh, dressed in the latest Tudor fashion.

# What would I eat and drink?

In Tudor times, you ate what your family could afford. As a poor child, your food was very plain. You mostly ate heavy, dark bread made from barley or rye, cheese, and a thick vegetable soup, called **pottage**. You had weak beer to drink.

There were no forks in Tudor times! People ate with knives and spoons, or with their fingers.

For most ordinary people, meat was a luxury. But if you came from a wealthy family, meat made up a large part of your diet. It came from deer, cows, pigs, wild boar, birds, and rabbits. You usually ate fresh meat, but some was **preserved** by rubbing salt into it. On Fridays, you ate fish instead of meat. You also ate white bread made from wheat.

Towards the end of Tudor times, people started to eat some new foods. Turkeys, potatoes, and tomatoes were brought back to England by explorers sailing to the New World of the Americas. Cauliflowers came from Asia.

Here is the Tudor kitchen in the palace of Hampton Court.

## SWEET TOOTH

Sugar was very expensive and you only had sweets if you were rich. A favourite treat was marzipan, a paste made from almonds and sugar. It was made into the shapes of castles, animals, and fruit, and decorated with real gold.

# Would I go to school?

In Tudor times, you only went to school if your parents were wealthy. Most poor people could not afford school **fees** and expected their children to go to work. Boys and girls from the richest families were educated by tutors (private teachers) at home.

It was mostly boys who went to school. They began at about the age of four. This was a kind of nursery school, called a "petty" school. At seven, they moved to grammar school. These schools got their name because the pupils learnt Latin grammar. They also studied Greek, mathematics, geography, and literature.

This is a picture of a classroom in a Tudor grammar school.

# The school day

The school day was very long. You started at seven in the morning and finished around five o'clock in the afternoon. You even went to school on Saturdays. Tudor teachers were very strict. If a pupil made a mistake, he was often beaten with a birch made out of sharp twigs.

Tudor children learned to write by copying from a horn book, like this one. It was a wooden paddle with a sheet of paper glued on and covered in cow's horn.

# UNIVERSITIES

There were two universities in England in Tudor times: Oxford and Cambridge. Only boys could attend. They studied arts, law, medicine, or theology (religion).

# What would I do when I grew up?

Most Tudor people lived in the countryside and worked as farmers. Children were expected to help in the fields from the age of about seven. You might do a job such as scaring birds away from the crops, or helping to pick fruit.

Here village families are bringing in the harvest.

## MERCHANTS

Merchants bought goods and then sold them to other people. In Tudor times, exciting new goods, such as tobacco, were brought to England for the first time. Many merchants became very rich.

# Apprentices

If you wanted to learn a trade or craft, you had to become an **apprentice**. Most apprentices were boys. You started around the age of 14. Apprentices were not paid for their work, but lived with the "master" (teacher) as part of his family. The training usually took about seven years and you had to obey the rules. You were not allowed to get married, or spend too much time in Tudor taverns!

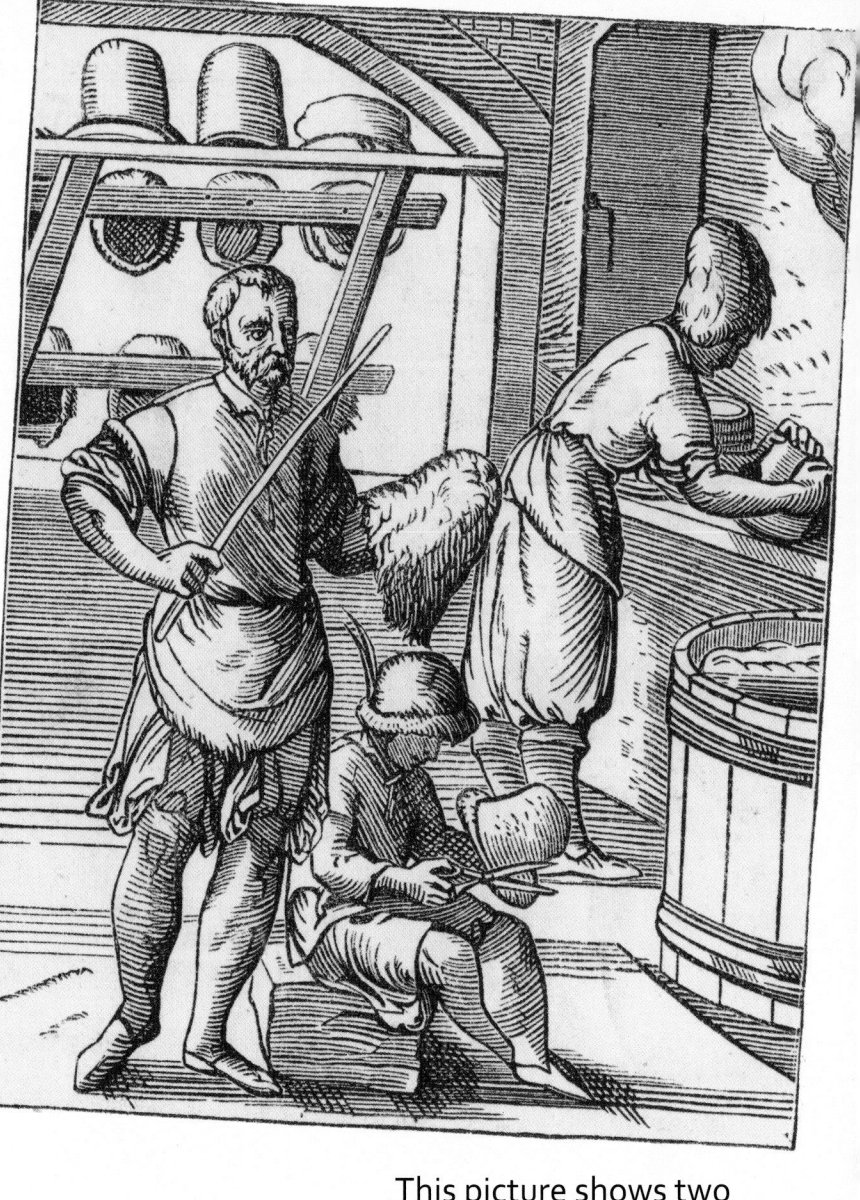

This picture shows two hat-makers with their apprentice.

# Running the house

Girls learnt how to run a household. In a poor family, you had to make the food for your household, including brewing ale and baking bread. In a well-off home, you were in charge of managing the servants and teaching the children.

# What would I believe?

At the beginning of Tudor times, almost everyone in England was a **Roman Catholic**. The **Pope** was head of the Church. This was a time of great religious change. New **Protestant** churches were starting up across Europe.

## Church of England

The Pope would not allow Henry VIII to get a divorce from his first wife, Catherine of Aragon. So Henry set up a new Church of England, and made himself its leader. He closed down the Roman Catholic **abbeys** and **monasteries** in England and seized all their buildings, land, and wealth.

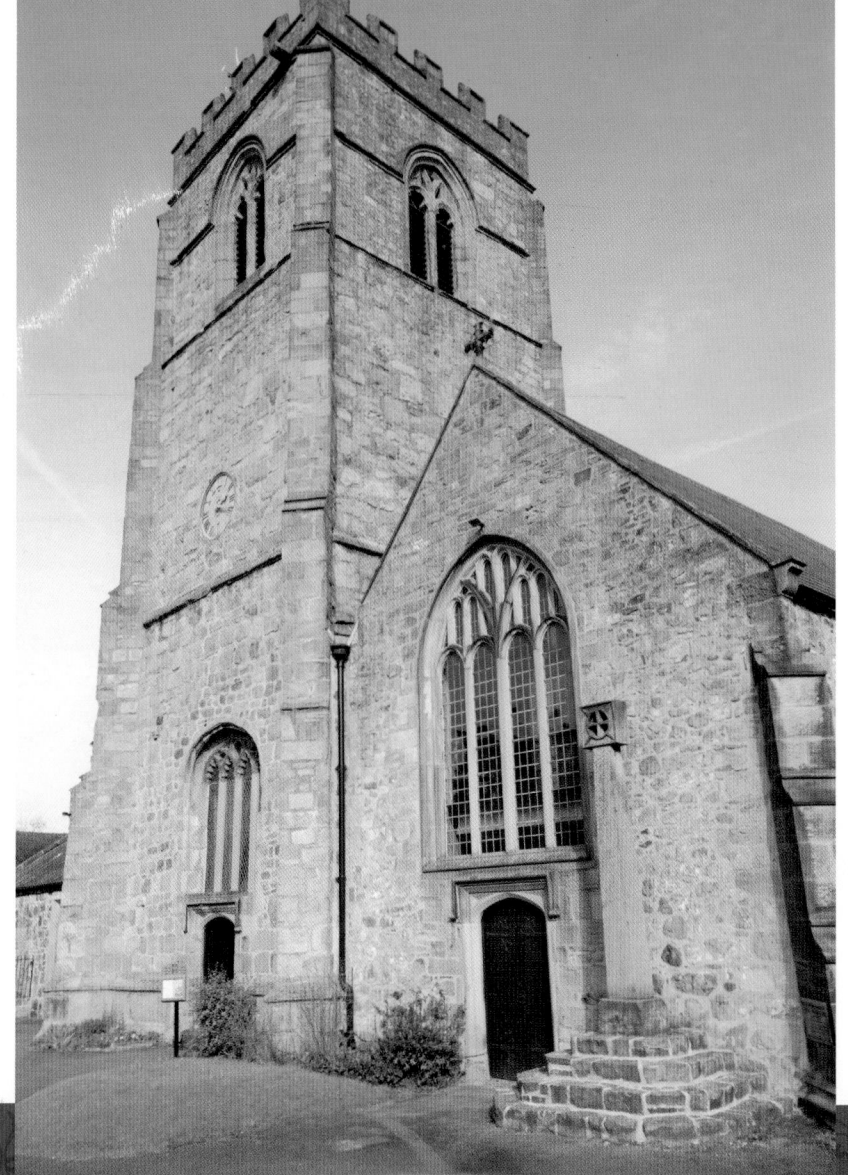

St Mary's Church in Chirk, Wrexham was used in Tudor times.

The Tudor kings and queens wanted to make ordinary people follow the same beliefs that they did. Under Henry's son Edward VI, England was a Protestant country. But Mary I, Henry's daughter by the wife he divorced, was Catholic, so the country became Catholic again. Many people were executed for refusing to change their beliefs.

## THE ENGLISH BIBLE

The Bible used by Roman Catholics was written in Latin, which only educated people could understand. In 1539, Henry VIII ordered a Bible in English to be put in every church. He wanted ordinary people to be able to hear and read the Bible in their own language.

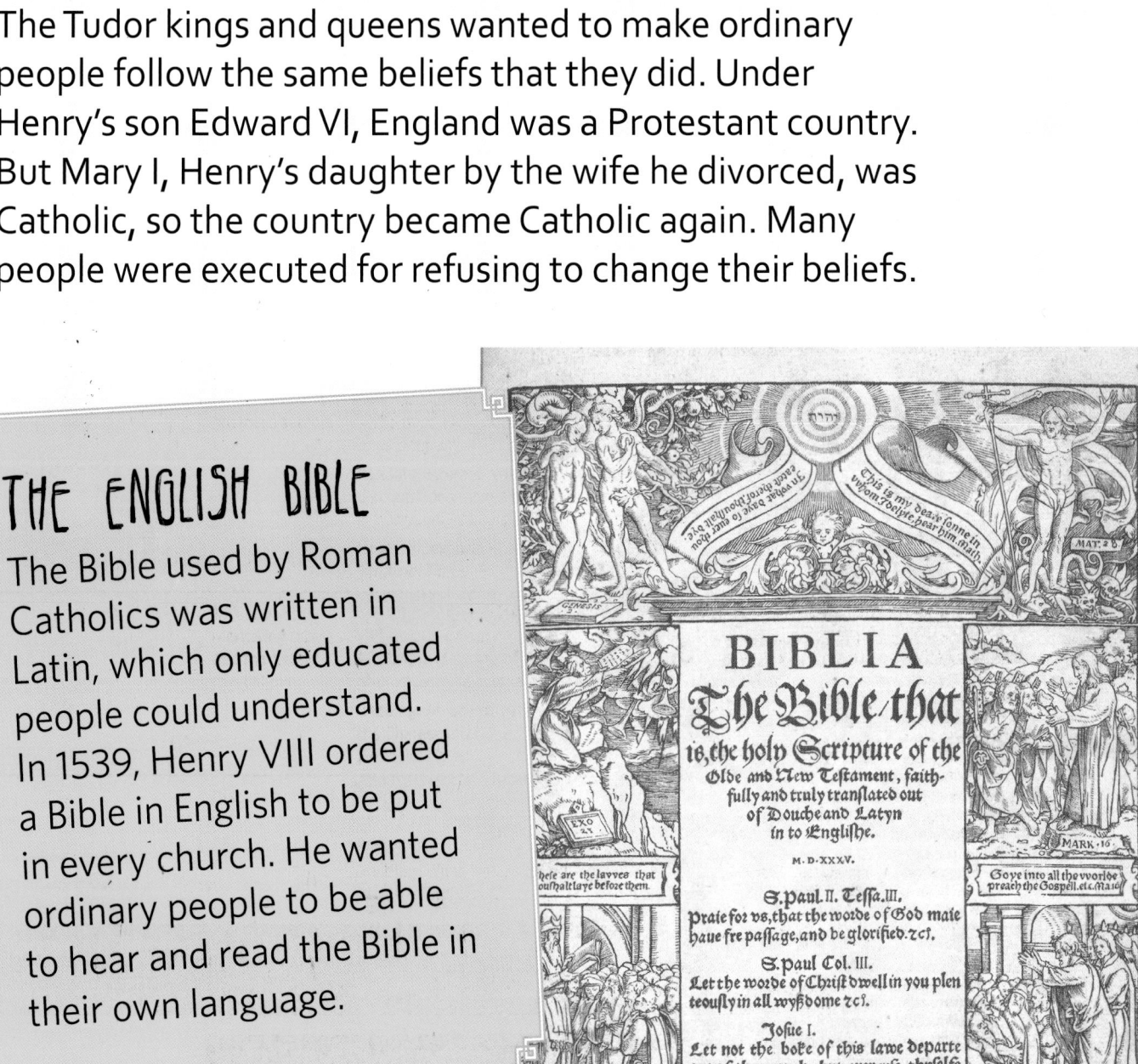

This is the title page of the first modern English translation of the Bible, dating from 1535.

# How would I have fun?

Tudor children loved to play with toys, such as dolls, hoops, and balls. Dolls made from wood were called Bartholomew Babies. This is because they were sold at St Bartholomew's Fair, a big street market in London.

You might also play football with a ball made from an animal's bladder (a hollow organ in the body, like a bag, that stores wee), blown up with air. Football was a dangerous game in Tudor times. There were few rules and teams could be whole villages. The day-long game often ended in fights, and broken legs and arms! Other popular games were less dangerous. People played Nine Men's Morris, a board game that is a bit like noughts and crosses.

These boys are playing football at a Tudor grammar school.

Caption to come

A play is being staged at a model of Shakespeare's Globe Theatre.

# THEATRE-GOERS

As a treat, you might go to the theatre. In Elizabeth I's time, there were many theatres in London. Men and boys played all the parts, including the female ones, because women were not allowed to act. The most famous playwright was William Shakespeare. His plays, including *Romeo and Juliet* and *Hamlet*, were very popular.

Hunting was a popular sport. If your parents were nobles or **gentry,** you learnt how to hunt boar and deer on horseback. People also hunted with trained hawks.

# After the Tudors

Queen Elizabeth I never married. When she died in 1603, there were no children to take over the throne. The Tudor age came to an end. It was Elizabeth's relative, James Stuart, who became king.

Mary, Queen of Scots, was put on trial in 1587.

## MARY, QUEEN OF SCOTS

James I's mother was Mary, Queen of Scots. She was forced to flee to England in 1568 because of power struggles in Scotland. Elizabeth I took her prisoner and, eventually, in 1587, ordered Mary's execution.

James was the first Stuart king of England. He was already James VI of Scotland and was the first person to rule both England and Scotland.

# Changing times

The Tudor period was a time of great change. At home, cities such as London grew much bigger and there was a huge growth in trade and entertainment, with many new theatres built. There were major, often violent, changes in religion as England turned from being a **Catholic** to a **Protestant** country.

Further afield, British explorers sailed around the world and brought back new goods and foods. Their great journeys led the way for British settlers to start new lives across the Atlantic in America.

This is a portrait of James I of England.

# How do we know?

On 19 July 1545, King Henry VIII watched proudly as his favourite warship, the *Mary Rose*, sailed out from Portsmouth harbour to fight the French fleet. Then disaster struck. The mighty *Mary Rose* rolled over and started to sink. More than 435 years later, in 1982, the wreck was finally raised from the seabed. Thousands of objects belonging to the crew were also found. They give us an amazing look at life on board a Tudor warship.

Officers on the *Mary Rose* would have used fine pewter dishes, like these. Wooden items, like the tankard, would have been used by the rest of the crew.

This surgeon's chest was found on the *Mary Rose*. It contained medicine, surgical tools, a razor for shaving the crew members, and a bowl for collecting blood!

# Family tree

FAMILY TREES EXPLAINED!
Lines going down mean the person below was the child of the person above. So Elizabeth I was the daughter of Henry VIII.

## Tudor kings and queens

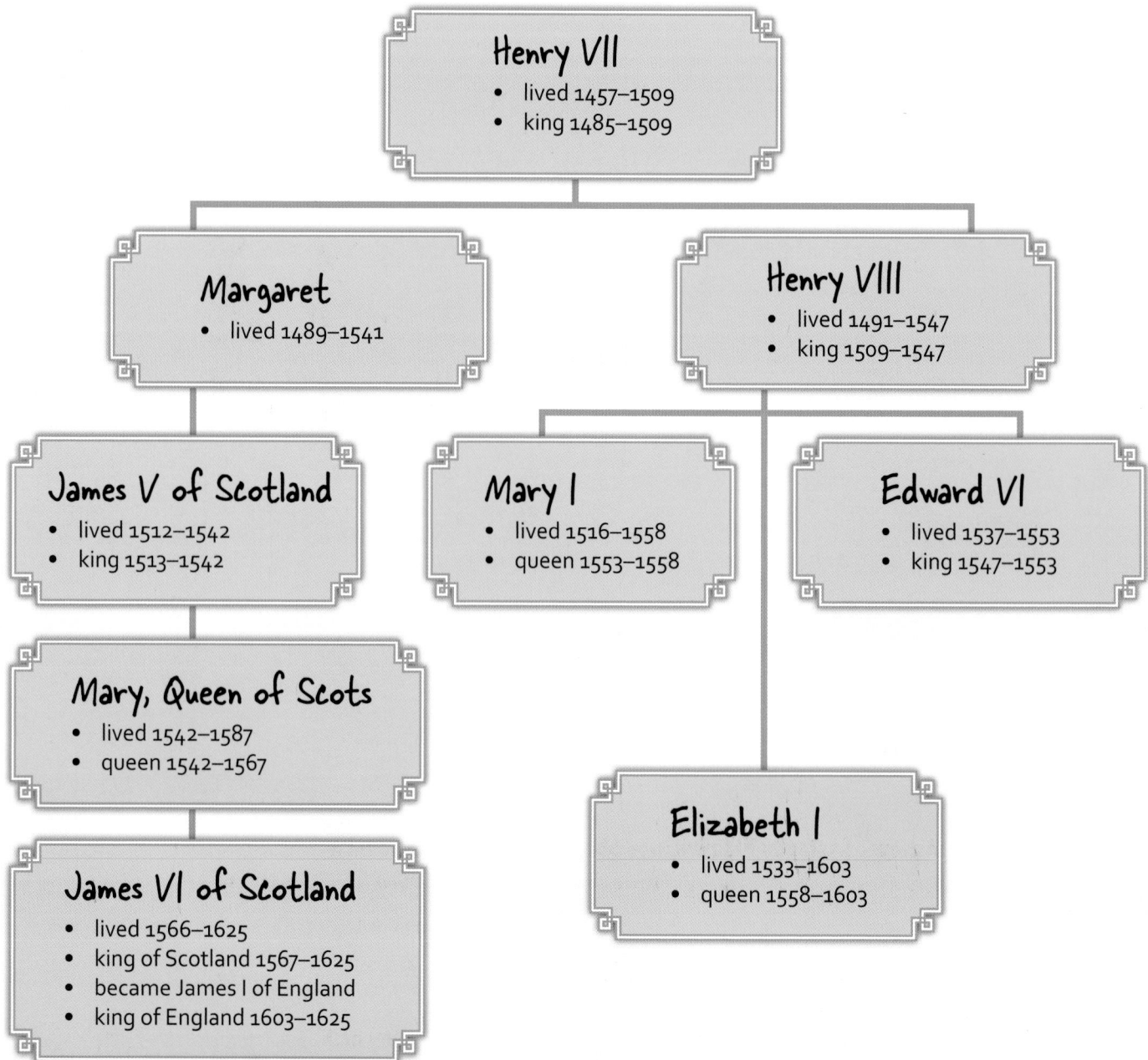

**Henry VII**
- lived 1457–1509
- king 1485–1509

**Margaret**
- lived 1489–1541

**Henry VIII**
- lived 1491–1547
- king 1509–1547

**James V of Scotland**
- lived 1512–1542
- king 1513–1542

**Mary I**
- lived 1516–1558
- queen 1553–1558

**Edward VI**
- lived 1537–1553
- king 1547–1553

**Mary, Queen of Scots**
- lived 1542–1587
- queen 1542–1567

**Elizabeth I**
- lived 1533–1603
- queen 1558–1603

**James VI of Scotland**
- lived 1566–1625
- king of Scotland 1567–1625
- became James I of England
- king of England 1603–1625

# Quiz

What do you know about life in Tudor times? Try this quiz to find out!

1. What was the Tudor emblem?
   **a** a red rose
   **b** a red and white rose
   **c** a white rose

2. What new foods came to England in Tudor times?
   **a** potato
   **b** tomato
   **c** carrot

3. What were Bartholomew Babies?
   **a** a type of sweet
   **b** a type of doll
   **c** a type of puppy

4. What would you do with a pair of hose?
   **a** use them to tie up your horse
   **b** use them to put out a fire
   **c** wear them on your legs

5. What was rich people's furniture made of?
   **a** oak
   **b** metal
   **c** plastic

**Answers**
1. b
2. a and b
3. b
4. c
5. a

# Glossary

**abbey** building where monks live and worship

**apprentice** person who is learning a trade

**breeches** short trousers

**court** place where a king or queen lives, together with their nobles and servants

**emblem** picture that represents a person or a family

**embroider** decorate cloth with coloured thread in different stitches

**fee** price paid for something

**gentry** wealthy landowners

**monarch** king or queen

**monastery** community of monks

**panelling** wall covering usually made out of wood

**Pope** head of the Roman Catholic Church, which is based in Rome, Italy

**pottage** type of thick soup made from oats and vegetables

**preserve** to prevent food from spoiling or going off

**Protestant** name given to Christians who began to question the teachings of the Roman Catholic Church in the 1500s, and demanded changes

**reign** time period a king or queen rules

**Roman Catholic** Church based in Rome, which has the Pope as its head

**vagrant** person without a home or regular work who wanders from place to place

# Find out more

## Books

Discover the Tudors (series), Moira Butterfield (Franklin Watts, 2013)

*Tudor* (Eyewitness), (Dorling Kindersley, 2011)

*Tudors* (Hail!), Philip Steele (Wayland, 2013)

*Tudors* (History Corner), Alice Harman (Wayland, 2012)

*Tudors* (Project History), Sally Hewitt (Franklin Watts, 2012)

## Websites

**www.museumoflondon.org.uk/Explore-online/Pocket-histories/tudor-life**
Find out about life in Tudor London on the Museum of London website.

**www.show.me.uk/topicpage/Tudors.html**
This website has information and fun activities about the Tudors from museums around Britain.

**www.tudorbritain.org**
With this interactive website, you take the part of a historian finding out about Tudor life through original documents and objects.

## Places to visit

There are many Tudor houses and homes to visit all over Britain. You can find out about them through the following organizations:

English Heritage
www.english-heritage.org.uk

The National Trust in England, Wales, and Northern Ireland
www.nationaltrust.org.uk

The National Trust of Scotland
www.nts.org.uk

# Index